W9-AKD-939

FLUTED VASE WITH PARROT EFFIGY LEGS, COLIMA
WARRIOR HEAD "HACHA" FORM OF VOLCANIC ROCK, CENTRAL VERACRUZ
CLASSIC SEATED ANIMAL, VOLCANIC ROCK. VERACRUZ
SEATED WARRIOR, JALISCO HOLLOW PAINTED CLAY
CLAY URN ZAPOTECAN FROM OAXACA
PAINTED CLAY WHISTLE SEATED PRIESTESS, ISLAND OF JAINA
HOLLOW PAINTED CLAY WHISTLE, SEATED PRIEST WITH FACIAL TATTOO, ISLAND OF JAINA
HOLLOW CLAY DOG, COLIMA
HOLLOW CLAY FRAGMENT CENTRAL VERACRUZ
EARTHENWARE DOG VESSEL, COLIMA
CLAY MASK COLIMA
HOLLOW CLAY SEATED MAN FROM COLIMA
HOLLOW CLAY SEATED MAN WITH BOWL AND RATTLE, COLIMA
HOLLOW CLAY SEATED FIGURE WITH DOG, COLIMA

BONE KNIFE WITH GOLD FOIL, GLYPHS
COPPER TURTLE FROM A NECKLACE
REMOJODAS, CENTRAL VERACRUZ
STANDING ARCHAIC STYLE FIGURE FROM TLATILCO, MEXICO CITY
EARLY WARRIOR, PAINTED CLAY, TOLTEC
POTTERY WARRIOR, PROBABLY MAYAN, A.D. 600-900
HOLLOW CLAY SEATED FIGURE, COLIMA
SEATED WOMAN HOLDING BOWL, HOLLOW CLAY, COLIMA
STYLIZED CERAMIC MASK
CLAY DANCER AND ACROBAT, PRE-CLASSIC, 1000 B.C.
BEADS
SEATED MAN WITH HELMET, HOLLOW PAINTED CLAY, NAYARIT
POT WITH EFFIGY HEADS, COLIMA
BEADS
BEADS
HOLLOW CLAY SEATED FIGURE, SHELL NECKLACE, COLIMA
TOY CROCODILE

Enchantment of America

MEXICO

By Frances E. Wood

Illustrations by Katherine Grace

CHILDRENS PRESS, Chicago

The author thanks Gilberto Espinosa of Albuquerque, New Mexico, whose scholarly research and interest in Mexico and the Spanish Southwest have made his suggestions for this book most helpful.

SECOND PRINTING
Library of Congress Catalog Card Number: 64-11106

Printed in the U.S.A.

Contents

The land

Location

Mexico, our sister republic on the south, is an enchanting land of mountains and deserts, golden sunshine and purple shadows, dense evergreen forests and tropical jungles.

Composed of twenty-nine states and two territories, the republic stretches between the southwestern United States—California, Arizona, New Mexico, and Texas—and Central America. The Rio Grande forms the entire boundary between Mexico and Texas. (Below El Paso, the Mexicans call this mighty river the *Rio Bravo;* north of El Paso, where it is entirely within the United States, they often refer to it as the *Rio del Norte*, or "River of the North.") The Pacific Ocean is on the west and the Gulf of Mexico on the east.

Narrowing to about 125 miles at the Isthmus of Tehuantepéc, southern Mexico widens again as it curls around the Gulf of Mexico and ends in the Yucatán Peninsula, which it shares with Guatemala and British Honduras. The Gulf of California separates the long, narrow peninsula of Lower, or Baja, California from the west coast of the mainland.

TIJUANA
BAJA CALIFORNIA
SONORA
CHIHUAHUA
COAHUIL
SINALOA
DURANGO
LA PAZ
MAZATLAN
ZACATECAS
SAN LUIS
NAYARIT
AGUAS CALIENTES
GUADALAJARA
GUANAJUATO
JALISCO
LAKE PATZCUARO
COLIMA
MICHOACAN
GUER
ACAPULCO
MEXICO

N
W
E
S
M
NUEVO
LEON
TAMAULIPAS
MATAMOROS
TAMPICO
POTOSI
QUERETARO
HIDALGO
VERA CRUZ
MEXICO
MEXICO CITY
MORELOS
TAXCO
PUEBLA
OAXACA
TEHUANTEPEC
CHIAPAS
TABASCO
CAMPECHE
YUCATAN
CHICHEN ITZA
UXMAL
YUCATAN PENINSULA
BRITISH HONDURAS
GUATEMALA
HONDURAS
EL SALVADOR

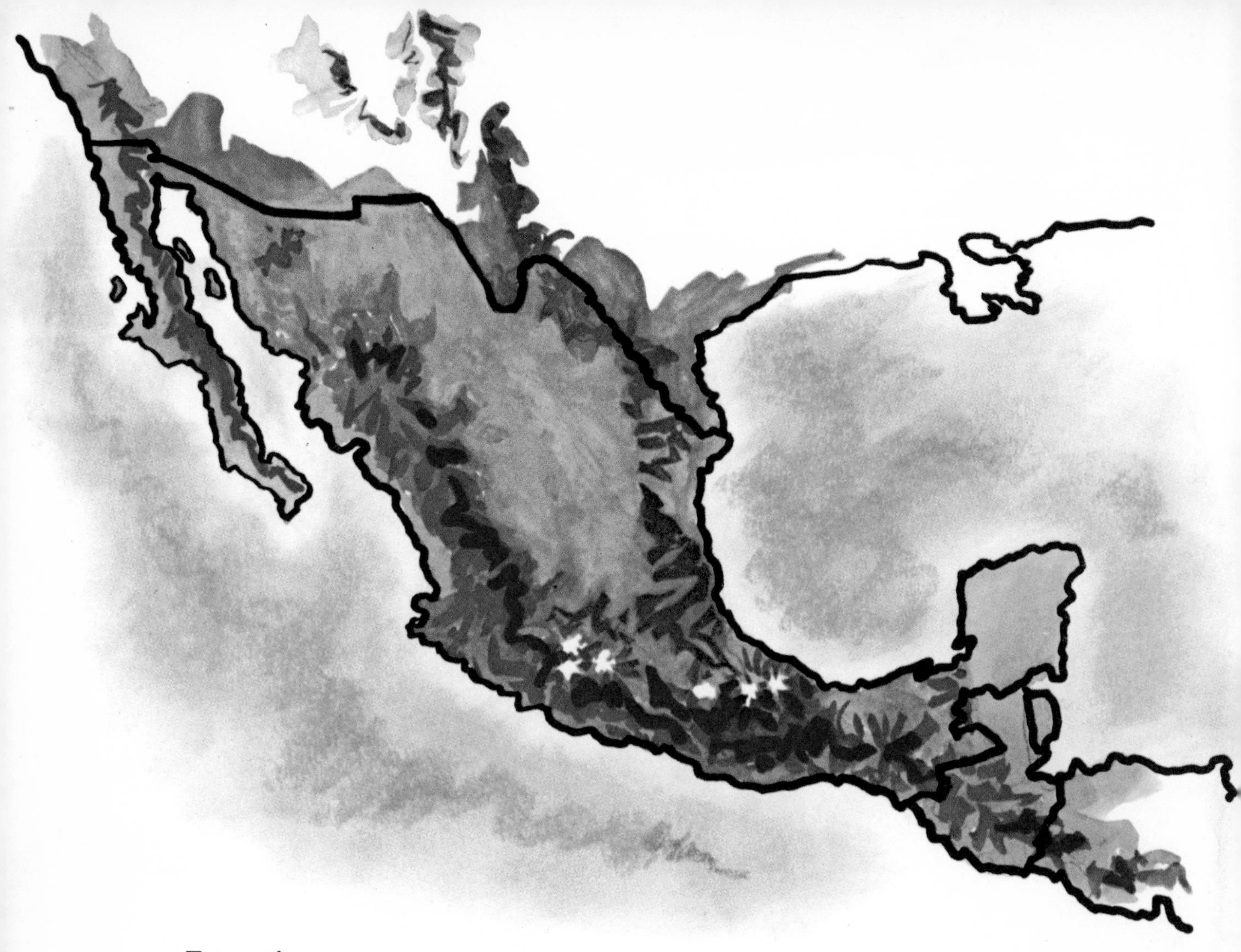

Formation

More than a hundred million years ago a great sea spread over much of North America, stretching from the Gulf of Mexico to the Arctic regions and covering most of Mexico. Through many millions of years, the earth rose and the sea retreated. Dinosaurs roamed North America, and the first birds appeared. Then the dinosaurs died out, and warm-blooded mammals took over the land.

About seventy million years ago, pressure inside the earth caused its crust to buckle and fold and push upward throughout western North America, and the Cordilleran mountain system was born. This included the great mass of mountains that covers three-fourths of Mexico

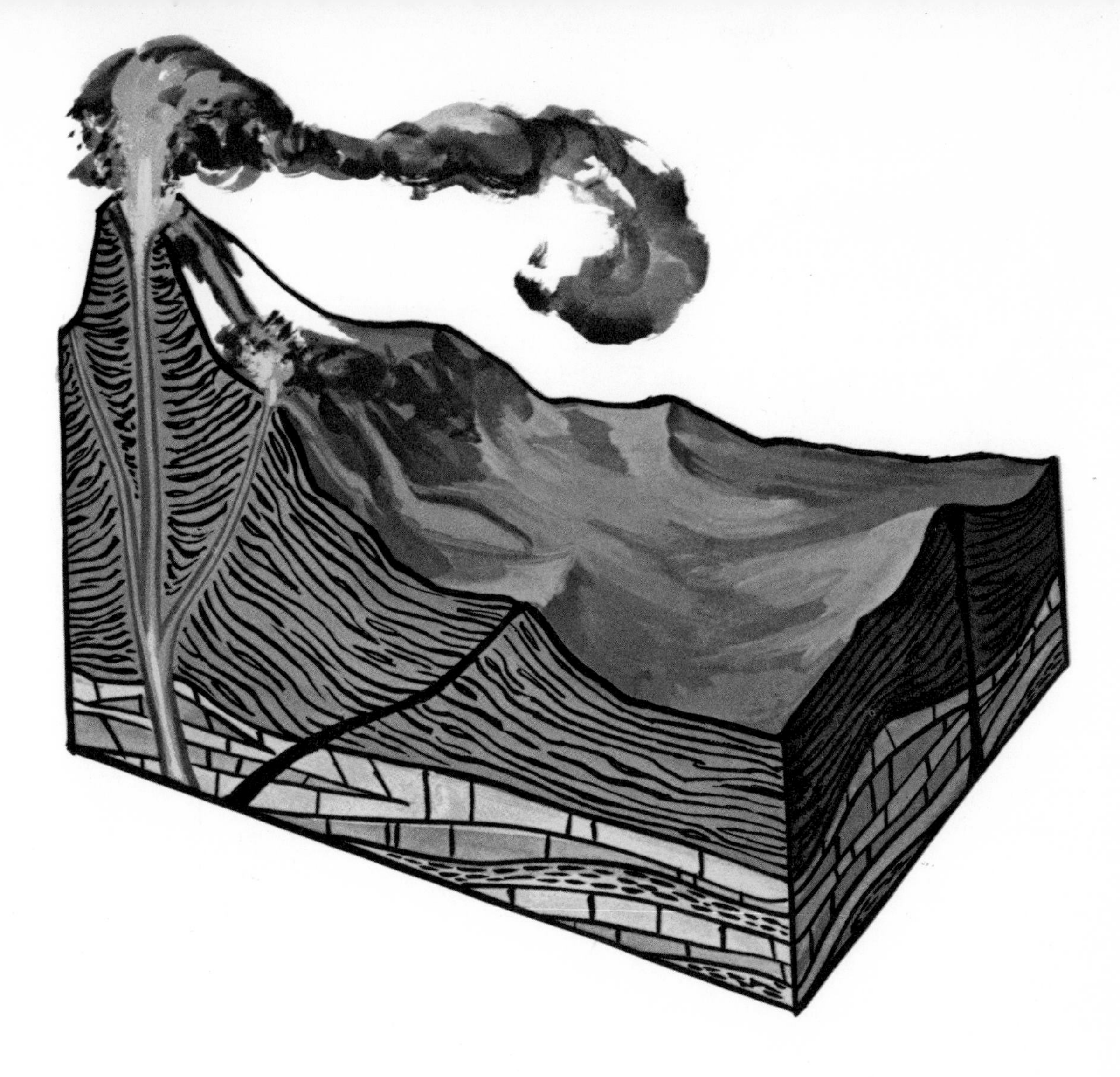

today. Molten rock pushed up through cracks in the rock and issued from the earth in the form of lava, and hot gases threw rocks and ash and cinders into the air, building up volcanic peaks. The highest peaks in Mexico were formed in this way, and the Central Plateau, through millions of years, was built up by lava flows.

The volcanoes of Mexico are a part of the row of active and extinct volcanoes, called the Pacific Ring of Fire, that almost encircles the Pacific Ocean. The volcanic peaks of the Cascade Range in the United States, which include Mount Lassen, Mount Hood, and Mount Rainier, are also a part of the Ring of Fire, as are the great volcanoes of Alaska.

Birth of a Volcano

There are numerous earth movements, or earthquakes, in Mexico today, and no one knows when a volcano may be born. The newest one is Paricutín, which started in a cornfield one day in February of 1943, while the owner was plowing his field. First, a thin wisp of what appeared to be smoke came through a crack in the earth. Then a deep rumbling was heard, and the earth shook. A larger crack opened up with a roar, and a stream of rocks exploded through the crack.

Although the people were terror stricken, they crowded around the cornfield to watch a new volcano in the making. With loud explosions, rocks flew high into the air and then fell back, building a cone-shaped pile higher and higher around the opening. In about a week, lava began flowing from a crack in the side of the cone. As the days and weeks passed, more and more lava flowed out; the cornfield was covered with rocks and lava, and the volcano became higher and wider. In the months and years that followed, two villages were swallowed up by the lava, and by 1952, when the volcano finally died, the cone had risen to a height of 1,350 feet.

Lay of the Land Today

Seen from the air, the surface of Mexico resembles a huge mass of crumpled parchment. Towering, snow-capped mountain ranges, the Sierra Madre Oriental (Eastern) and the Sierra Madre Occidental (Western) extend along each coast, with narrow coastal plains between the mountains and the sea. The high, rugged Central Plateau stretches between the mountain ranges.

Paricutín is in an east-west range of volcanic peaks that connects the Sierra Madre Occidental and the Sierra Madre Oriental and rims the southern edge of the Central Plateau. Popocatépetl and Ixtaccihuatl, twin volcanic peaks southwest of Mexico City, were lovers in Indian legend. Ixtaccihuatl, whose long profile resembles a sleeping woman covered by a mantle of snow, is extinct, but steam sometimes pours from the snow-capped crest of Popocatépetl. Highest peak in Mexico is Orizaba (18,851 feet), also called Citlaltepetl by the Indians.

The great Central Plateau ascends gradually from an altitude of about 3,600 feet in the north to more than 8,000 feet in the south. Part of the plateau is fairly level, but where it nears the southern mountains, the surface is crumpled into high ridges that enclose basins and valleys. One of the most beautiful of these is the Valley of Mexico, containing Mexico City and many smaller towns and villages.

Chapala, Mexico's largest lake, lies in an intermountain basin in the southwestern corner of the plateau, and the highly scenic Lakes Patzcuaro and Cuitzeo are between Lake Chapala and Mexico City. The lakes of Texcoco, Xochimilco, and Chalco, in the Valley of Mexico, are the remnants of ancient lakes that were the center of famous prehistoric Indian civilizations.

The extreme southern part of Mexico is a jumble of mountains, interspersed with steep-walled little valleys. Isolated tribes of Indians, each tribe speaking a different language, live in many of these little valleys. The only areas near sea level are the coastal plains and the flat Peninsula of Yucatán, which lies between the Gulf of Mexico and the Caribbean Sea.

Mexico has numerous unnavigable rivers, many of which become raging torrents during the rainy season and then almost dry up. A few that flow into the Gulf of Mexico, such as the Pánuco and the Coatza-coalcos, are navigable for a short distance.

Climate

Although the Tropic of Cancer crosses Mexico and most of the country lies in the subtropics or the tropics, it has a great variety of climate, due to the differences in altitude. The northern part of the Central Plateau has a hot, dry desert climate. As we travel southward on the plateau, the altitude becomes higher and higher, and the climate, instead of being hot, as we would expect when we near the tropics, becomes temperate.

The Valley of Mexico, although it lies in the tropical zone, south of the Tropic of Cancer, has a mild year-round climate, with cool nights and pleasant days. That is because the altitude here is more than 7,000 feet. Many of the mountain peaks that surround the Central Plateau are snow-capped throughout the year. A hot, humid, tropical climate prevails along the narrow coastal plains and the Peninsula of Yucatán.

Rainfall varies, too, from less than ten inches a year in the dry north to as much as ninety inches along the humid coast. Mexico has only two seasons—the rainy season, from June to October, and the dry, from November to May.

Things to think about

Trace the "Ring of Fire" on a world globe, and tell what far-distant volcanoes it includes.

How does the Central Plateau of Mexico differ from the highlands of the western United States!

Tell how variations in climate and rainfall are caused by differences in altitude of the land.

How did the topography of Mexico influence a difference in languages and customs of the early peoples?

People come to Mexico

The First People

It is not known exactly when the first people came to Mexico. A man's bones, found near the village of Tepexpán, in the Valley of Mexico, are thought to be more than 10,000 years old. A bone from an extinct llama species—carved to resemble the face of another wild animal—which was dug up near Mexico City, is believed to be more than 11,000 years old. But the most exciting discovery of all is a recent find, near Puebla, of the bone of a mastodon which is covered with pictures of mastodons, camels, and other prehistoric animals. Scientists believe that these pictures were carved on the bone when it was fresh, at least 30,000 years ago.

New discoveries, such as this one, are constantly changing our thinking concerning the age of man in the New World. But, even though we don't know for sure just *when* man first came to this continent, scientists are pretty well agreed as to *how* he came. At the time the pictures were carved on the mastodon bone, more than half of North America was covered by great ice sheets which stretched down from the Arctic regions to what is now northern United States. Only a few areas were free from ice—Alaska and the Mackenzie River valley in Canada, and a narrow corridor along the east flank of the Rocky Mountains. So much water was locked up in the great ice sheets on land that the ocean was two to three hundred feet lower than it is now, and Bering Strait, which is only 150 feet deep, was an isthmus, or land bridge, between Alaska and Siberia.

The Ice Age had started in North America a million years or more ago. At least four times during this period, long fingers of ice had reached down from the north into the middle of the continent and then retreated again. Between the times of retreat and advance, the climate became mild again and vegetation flourished, only to be wiped out by the next advance of ice.

During the Ice Age, numerous mammals, many of them huge in size, roamed North America—mammoths, mastodons, giant bison, bear, deer, camels, horses, saber-toothed cats, giant beavers, ground sloths, and many other kinds of animals. Some were native to North America; some came up from South America; others crossed the land bridge between Alaska and Siberia. These animals crowded into the southern areas of the continent, including Mexico, when the ice moved down. Only the more hardy ones, such as the mammoths and mastodons, fed along the edges of the ice.

Mammoths and mastodons also lived in Mexico, along with horses, camels, rhinoceroses, beavers, enormous vultures, and many other animals. The bones of a huge cat, larger than the biggest tiger, were found in the Valley of Mexico. These cats preyed on the horses and camels and other animals.

It is thought that, during the last advance of the ice, possibly 30,000 years ago, the first people came to the New World, crossing into Alaska by means of the land bridge from Siberia. No doubt they were hunters, following the animals into a green Alaska, which, unlike Siberia, was free from ice. As more and more people came, through hundreds and even thousands of years, they gradually moved along through the Mackenzie River valley and along the eastern foot of the mountains until they had cleared the ice sheets.

Some of the people turned east and some west, wherever the land was free from ice. Others went to Mexico, and still others continued south until, through the years, they reached the southernmost tip of South America. By the time the Ice Age ended, probably less than 10,000 years ago, people had populated the New World from end to end of North and South America. Although there were many different peoples, speaking quite different languages, we call all of the first Americans "Indians," because that is what Christopher Columbus named the inhabitants when he came to the shores of the New World and thought he had reached the coast of India.

The Indians, 10,000 years ago, did not have bows and arrows, and they had not learned to domesticate animals. The only use they knew for the horse was to kill and eat it.

They did know about fire, and their progress through the Americas has been traced by the charred remains of campfires and the bones of animals which they cooked and ate, along with the spearheads with which they had killed the animals. All of these have been dug up through many layers of earth or found in caves in which the wandering hunters took refuge.

By the end of the Ice Age most of the large mammals of that period had vanished from this continent. The horse, which was a native of North America, became extinct in the New World. Fortunately, some of the horses had migrated to Asia over the land bridge, but they did not reappear in their native land until domesticated horses were brought to Mexico by the Spaniards many thousands of years later.

When big game was no longer available to the hunters, the people had to depend for food on whatever small game they could find and on seeds and nuts and fruit and the roots of plants. Instead of following the wandering herds, as they had done in earlier times, they searched for areas where plants grew that would give them food. Some of the tribes of Indians that went to Mexico stopped in the northern part; others settled on the shores of a great salt lake in the fertile, volcano-ringed Valley of Mexico; still others went on to the rain forests of southern Mexico and the gulf coast.

For centuries the people fished, hunted what game there was, and gathered wild grains and fruits, no doubt moving from the lowlands to the highlands and back with the changing seasons. Eventually, someone discovered that if he watered some of the wild plants in his vicinity and stirred up the earth around them, they would produce more food for him. Then, gradually, people realized that they could plant some of the best seeds and grow even better plants. So they began cultivating little garden patches of such vegetables as beans and squash and, finally, the plant which we know as corn.

The Mayas

It is not known exactly where or when the Indians first started raising corn—it might have been in Mexico or in Central America, or in both places at about the same time. But the cultivation of this life-giving grain spread far and wide among the farming peoples of the New World and gave rise to ancient civilizations in Mexico and Central and South America that were unparalleled in their brilliance and magnificence. One of the greatest of these civilizations was that of the Mayas.

This civilization had its beginnings in the jungles of what is now Guatemala, Honduras, and southern Mexico at least 2,000 years before the birth of Christ, when the ancestors of the Mayas began their first crude cultivation of corn. Their method of clearing the land was to kill the trees by girdling them and then burning them off. When the planting season arrived, they dropped the seeds into holes which they made with a "planting stick," sharpened on one end to a fine point.

Gradually, through the centuries, the Mayas learned many other things. They grew other plants for food, such as squash and beans, and gourds for carrying water, and cotton. They learned to spin and weave and to make pottery, which became finer and finer as the years passed.

Little by little they developed the arts of ceramics and painting and sculpture and architecture to an amazing degree.

The Mayas were deeply religious and worshiped many gods—personifications of animals of the forest, such as the serpent and the jaguar, and the physical elements that made agriculture possible, especially the sun and the wind and the rain. Their priests studied the stars and developed, from the movements of the solar system, an accurate calendar. In their calculations, they made use of the zero a thousand years before the Hindus used it in India.

By 200 A.D., nearly thirteen centuries before Columbus planted the Spanish flag in the New World, the Mayan civilization was flourishing. Gleaming "cities" arose on clearings in the jungle. These were not cities as we know them, but ceremonial centers, consisting of a central plaza, surrounded by temples on towering pyramids and palaces in which the priests and nobles lived. Fanning out in all directions from the ceremonial centers and reaching to the edge of the ever-encroaching jungle, were the thatch-roofed huts of the common people and their patches of corn and other vegetables. On the central plazas of the ceremonial centers, it is likely that there were also open-air markets, for the Mayas not only traded among themselves, but it is probable that they also traded with other Indian groups living along the gulf coast and in the Valley of Mexico, as well as in Central America.

For six hundred years the Mayan civilization was at the height of its glory. Without domestic animals or metal farming implements or wheeled vehicles, the common people raised enough corn to feed the populace and at the same time performed the tremendous labor that was necessary to erect the great pyramids and public buildings, which had beautiful frescoes, carvings, and sculptures on the outside walls and colorful murals on the inside. With all this, the people found time to make fine pottery and jewelry, to model tiny, lifelike figures from clay or carve them from jade, and to do exquisite featherwork.

Even more extraordinary was the study of astronomy and mathematics which the priests pursued. Apparently without telescopes or other instruments, they were able to work out extremely accurate solar and religious calendars from the movements of the sun, moon, stars, and

MAYAN
MARKET

planets, especially the planet Venus, which they called the Great Star.

They could accurately predict the coming of comets and solar eclipses for many years ahead; and they could calculate the dates each year of the equinoxes and solstices and tell the farmers when to plant their crops and carry on their other activities. The common people, who did not understand these things, looked upon the priests as beings who had been endowed by the gods with supernatural powers.

The priests worked out a system of picture writing, called hieroglyphics, and a numbering system, which was based on the concept of 20 instead of 10, on which our numbering system is based. In writing numbers, they used a system of dots and bars, in which each dot equaled one and each bar equaled five:

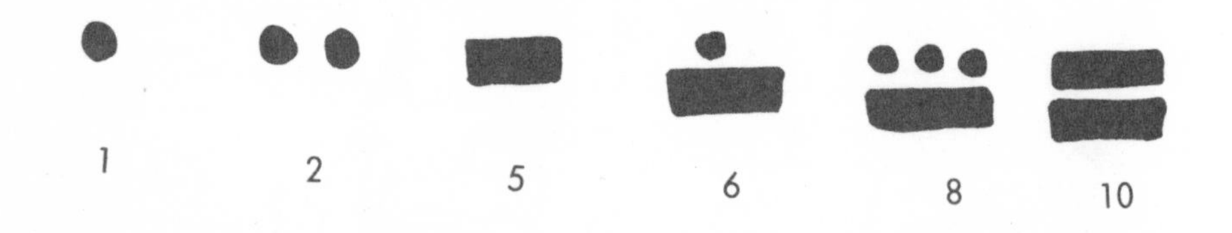

and so on through 19, which was three bars surmounted by four dots:

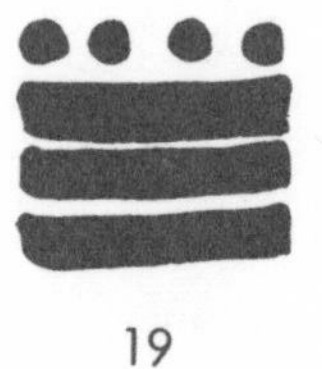

19

Higher numbers were represented by position, similar to our decimal system, except that they were placed one above another instead of horizontally. The Mayas also had picture words, or glyphs, for their numbers, just as we often spell out the words instead of using figures. Frequently, especially with figures larger than 19, they combined the dots and bars with the pictures. Zero was represented by the picture of a shell.

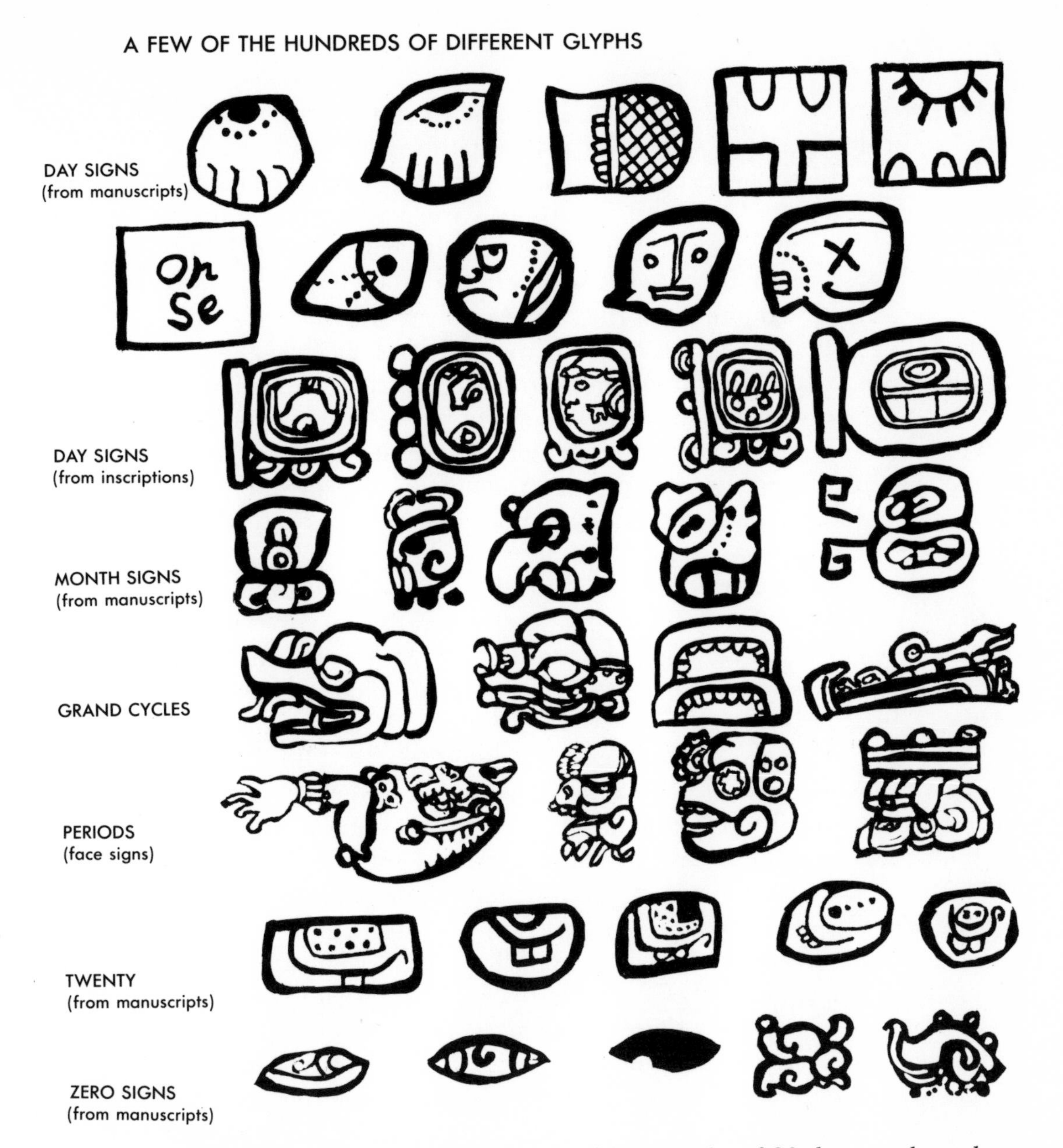

The Mayan calendar consisted of 18 months of 20 days each and one of five days, which was considered a very unlucky period. This calendar went through a cycle of 52 years, corresponding somewhat to our century of 100 years. The Mayas also had a sacred year of 260 days.

There were many holy days on the calendar when the people flocked to the central plaza to watch their priests perform colorful religious rites in a haze of copal incense, and to dance and sing in the ceremonials and festivals. The priests themselves were a dazzling sight in their feather robes and jaguar skins, adorned with costly ornaments of jade and shells. From their brightly painted masks and headpieces floated the long, green plumes of the sacred quetzal bird.

All the things that the priests learned from the stars, all the calendars and the mathematical equations they worked out, their predictions of eclipses and comets, were set down in books, along with the history and literature of the Mayas. These books, which were made from long strips of paper pounded from the bark of trees and covered with white paint, were handed down from generation to generation of priests and nobles, since the common people could not read.

Also, to mark the passing of certain intervals of time or to commemorate special dates or events of religious significance, shafts, or "stelae," of stone were set up in ceremonial centers. Each stele was beautifully carved with pictures and dates representing the event it commemorated.

This six-hundred-year period in the history of the Mayas, usually called the Classic Age, is also known as that of the Old Empire, although the Mayas did not have an empire in the real sense of the word. Each community was ruled by its priests and nobles, and, so far as is known, there was no central ruler or government.

The end of the Classic Age in Mayan history is shrouded in mystery. Between 800 and 900 A.D. (some authorities give the date as 600–900 A.D.) the Mayas abandoned their shining cities and went away, and the jungle closed in once more over the proud temples and palaces.

Hundreds of years later, many of their ruins, crumbling but still proud, were discovered in the jungles of Guatemala and Honduras and at Palenque and Bonampák, in Mexico. Scientists were able to piece out some of the people's story from the carvings and murals on the buildings, from the dates and hieroglyphics on the stelae, and from the artifacts found in the ruins. But nowhere was there anything to tell the searchers why the people had left or where they had gone. Scientists believe that hundreds, perhaps thousands, of other ruins remain hidden

BALL
COURT,
CHICHEN ITZA

and unexplored in the jungles. Perhaps the answer will be found in one of these lost ruins.

It may be that the ruins of Dzibilchaltún, near the northern coast of Yucatán, contain the answer, but only a little of this lost city has as yet been excavated. The city is so large and its buildings so badly crumbled that it may be years before its story can be revealed. Investigators believe, however, that this once-great city may have been founded one to two thousand years before the birth of Christ and was still inhabited at the time of the Spanish conquest in the sixteenth century A.D.

While the exodus from the Mayan cities of the Classic Age was taking place, other Mayan cities were developing in northern Yucatán. Again the gleaming white buildings of the Mayan ceremonial centers rose from the jungles, this time on the flat, hot peninsula of Yucatán. By the start of the eleventh century, Mayan culture had reached or exceeded that of the Classic Age. Most powerful of these cities were Chichén Itzá, Mayapán, and Uxmál.

About 1200 A.D. (some authorities give 1000 A.D.) the Toltecs from central Mexico invaded Yucatán and occupied Chichén Itzá. The architecture and other arts of the newcomers, as well as their customs and religion, greatly influenced the development of the city, and for the next two hundred years Chichén Itzá flourished as the holy city of Kukulcán, the Mayan name for Quetzalcoatl, the highest god of central Mexico. The feathered serpent, symbol of Quetzalcoatl, appears on many of the temples and other public buildings that were erected during this period.

Chichén Itzá had two large wells, or "cenotes," which are natural limestone sinkholes filled with fresh water. One of these, the Xtolóc Well, supplied the city with water. The other was the famous Well of Sacrifice, the mecca of worshipers from all over Mayaland, who came to throw in their most prized possessions as offerings to the gods. In times of drought, a beautiful maiden was also hurled into the well in an attempt to appease the rain god, for the Toltecs had brought to the Mayas their belief in human sacrifice.

After their civilization had risen to a new and brilliant height, civil war broke out about the middle of the fifteenth century, and the people

WELL OF
SACRIFICE

again abandoned their beautiful cities and allowed the jungle to creep over them once more. The inhabitants scattered. Some went to the highlands of Guatemala; others built new cities on the Yucatán Peninsula, which fell easy prey to the Spaniards when they invaded the area less than a century later.

The Spanish priests tore down the Mayan temples and burned their books, as instruments of the devil. Only three books were saved from destruction and taken to Europe, probably by Spanish soldiers. The story of a fabulous civilization has been put together from these books, from the ruins that have been uncovered in the jungles, and from the legends that have been handed down by word of mouth from generation to generation and are retold by the present-day Mayas.

Other Prehistoric Civilizations

But the Mayan civilization was only one of the numerous prehistoric Indian cultures that flourished in southern and central Mexico; all were dependent on the cultivation of corn and all had their gods and their temples and their calendars based on a 52-year cycle. The Olmecs, along the southern gulf coast, transported 30-ton blocks of basalt—no one knows how—sixty miles to their capital at La Venta and carved them into gigantic, startlingly realistic human heads. Northwest of La Venta, in their city of Tajín, the Totonacs worshiped at their seven-tiered Temple of Niches, so named because of the many niches set into the walls, in each of which, no doubt, an idol once stood. The Zapotecs built their beautiful mountain-top city of Monte Albán in Oaxaca and eventually lost it to the Mixtecs.

In the Valley of Mexico (then called Anáhuac) other Indians were building the city of Teotihuacán, whose mystery-shrouded ruins, north of Mexico City, are now a favorite tourist attraction. Arranged along a paved road, called the Street of the Dead, are the magnificent Pyramids of the Sun and the Moon, along with many other stone pyramids, on whose flattened summits wooden temples once stood. At one end of the road is the Temple of Quetzalcoatl, from whose beautifully carved

TEMPLES,
TEOTIHUACAN

walls project the heads of the plumed serpent. Apparently, worship of the god Quetzalcoatl prevailed throughout Mexico, as did also the practice of human sacrifice. Teotihuacán was destroyed about the beginning of the ninth century, possibly by the Toltecs, who moved into the valley from the north and built their own city of Tula, some miles away. The ruins of this city are marked by huge carved figures that once supported the roofs of the Toltec temples.

TULA

The Aztecs

The Aztecs (also called Mexicas), a wandering, barbarous tribe of Indians, arrived in the Valley of Mexico sometime during the thirteenth century, and for a time moved from place to place in the valley, absorbing the culture of the peoples who had arrived before them. According to prophecy, they were to make their home on the spot where they found an eagle, surrounded by cactus, holding a serpent in his beak. The symbol of the eagle and the serpent, which tradition says the Aztecs saw on a marshy island in Lake Texcoco now appears on the seal of Mexico and on the national flag.

The Aztecs settled on this island and a neighboring one about 1325 and, having adopted the customs and calendars and religion of their neighbors, they built magnificent stone pyramids and temples to their war god Huitzilopochtli, to the white god Quetzalcoatl, and to various other deities.

The island city, named Tenochtitlán, grew rapidly, and the Aztecs reclaimed swamplands and enlarged the islands, covering them with beautiful palaces and other buildings and connecting them to the mainland with several great causeways. In time they absorbed or subjugated all the other communities in the Valley of Mexico and surrounding areas, including southern Mexico and the gulf coastal plain, and ruled them with an iron hand from the capital city of Tenochtitlán.

When the Spaniards arrived in 1519, they found a shining city in a lake, with dazzling buildings and colorful floating gardens, which the Aztecs had made by heaping mud from the bottom of the lake onto rafts. Flower- and vegetable-laden canoes traveled along canals between the floating gardens, on their way to market. In addition to the flower and food stalls in the great public market, there were pottery-makers, basket-weavers, feather-workers, carvers, metal-workers, and many other artisans who made and sold their wares on the spot. There were also products brought from all over Mexico and from Central America. Elsewhere in the city, the warehouses of the emperor and the warrior-nobles were filled with gold and silver and other treasures that had been exacted as tribute from the many subjugated states.

Dominating the city were the gleaming religious temples, whose steps ran red with blood of sacrificial victims, for the Aztecs had adopted with enthusiasm their neighbors' belief in human sacrifice. Most of the victims were war prisoners, and a warrior's standing in the community depended on the number of prisoners he was able to capture for the sacrificial rites.

Coming of the Spaniards

The Spaniards, five hundred men and sixteen horses from the Spanish settlements in Cuba, had first landed on an island off the shore of Yucatán. Led by an intelligent and fearless young captain named Hernán Cortés, they subdued the frightened Indians, who had never before seen horses.

When Cortés left the island, he took with him a Spanish soldier, named Aguilar, who had been shipwrecked on the Yucatán coast eight years before, and a slave girl called Marina by the Spaniards. Both served Cortés as interpreters, and Marina proved to be invaluable as a guide, for she was well acquainted with the Aztec empire. She also was able to persuade many of the Indian communities along the way who hated Aztec tyranny to join the Spanish forces.

Even so, the Spaniards and their Indian allies were vastly outnumbered, and, in spite of their horses and guns, the Aztecs could easily

SPANISH
SOLDIERS

have annihilated them, but when the emperor, Montezuma II, heard of the white men's approach, he thought that Cortés was the white god Quetzalcoatl returning according to prophecy. So the emperor greeted Cortés with valuable presents and installed him in a palace near Montezuma's own. Then Cortés repaid the Aztecs' hospitality by holding the emperor and his nobles as prisoners and taking over the rule of the city himself.

This lasted for several months, and then Cortés left the city to meet a fresh force of Spanish soldiers that had landed on the coast. When he returned, he found that the officer he had left in charge had massacred a group of Aztecs who were celebrating a religious rite at one of their temples. The remaining Aztecs, aroused to fury, turned on the soldiers and, by holding them under heavy siege, were slowly starving them to death. Cortés forced Montezuma to address the infuriated citizens from a balcony and try to conciliate them, but his angry subjects promptly stoned him to death.

Cortés realized that he and his soldiers had better leave Tenochtitlán, and they tried to withdraw quietly at night over one of the causeways, carrying much of the city's treasure with them. But the Aztecs opened the drawbridge in the causeway, and the Spaniards had to swim to land. Many of them, heavily laden with gold and silver, sank to the bottom of the lake and drowned. Many more were killed by the Indians when they reached land.

Within six months Cortés had raised another force of Spanish soldiers, reinforced by many Indian allies, and, with horses and cannon, again marched against the Aztec capital. When Tenochtitlán finally surrendered on August 13, 1521, Cortés destroyed it and founded Mexico City on its ruins.

The Spaniards had stripped the Aztec city of its gold and silver and jewels and sent most of them to Spain. But even now, when excavations are made for new buildings in Mexico City or its environs, valuable relics of the lost city of Tenochtitlán are sometimes turned up. A highly prized relic is the famous Aztec Calendar Stone, a stone disc weighing more than twenty tons, which was dug up in 1790 and is now in the National Museum of Anthropology, in Mexico City. In the center of

the stone is engraved the face of the sun god, and surrounding him are the hieroglyphics representing the days and months and years of the Aztec calendar.

For three hundred years Mexico was under Spanish rule. Spain imposed its language, its religion, and its laws on "New Spain," as Mexico was called. The temples of the people were torn down as abodes of the devil, and churches or cathedrals were built on the spots where the temples had stood. The first church in North America was built on the ruins of the great Temple of Huitzilopochtli. Many of the Indians were burned as heretics or sold into slavery. The Church took over much of the land, and most of what remained was possessed by influential Spaniards, whose vast holdings were known as haciendas. The Indians were forced to work on the land and in the mines under a system that was little better than slavery. Many of them died of small-pox and other diseases that the white man brought to the New World.

On the other hand, there were the gentle Franciscan monks who worked among the Indians. By kindness rather than force, the monks were able to win the Indians to Catholicism.

Bartholomé de las Casas, Apostle of the Indians, did much to better their condition.

Independence from Spain

With the passing of the years and the intermarriage of the Spanish and the Indians, a new class of people, the "mestizos," became prominent. Inspired by the example of the United States, the mestizos, who had the stoicism of the Indian and the independence of the Spaniard, joined with the Mexican-born Spaniards in a freedom movement that spread throughout Mexico. A leader in the movement was Miguel Hidalgo y Costilla, a Catholic priest with a great compassion for the Indians; and his home, in the village of Dolores, was the scene of secret meetings of the revolutionaries, who were encouraged by Napoleon's occupation of Spain.

Early in the morning of September 16, 1810, Father Hidalgo rang his church bell long and loud, summoning his people to fight for their independence. Today the bell, Mexico's "Liberty Bell," hangs above the central portal of the National Palace in Mexico City. Every year, on the night of September 15, the eve of the Mexican Independence Day, the people crowd into the central plaza to hear their President ring the bell and repeat the words of Father Hidalgo's *Grito de Dolores*: "Long live our Lady of Guadalupe: And death to the Spaniards!" At the same time, the *Grito* is reenacted in every city and town of Mexico.

Father Hidalgo, after some months, was captured and executed by the royalist forces, but the flame he had kindled burned on. A mestizo priest named José María Morelos rose to leadership, gained control of a large portion of Mexico, and declared the independence of his country at the Congress of Chilpancingo before he, too, was captured and executed in 1815.

Augustín de Itúrbide, a colonel in the Spanish army, was commissioned to crush the remaining rebel forces. Instead, he joined the patriots, and on February 4, 1821, proclaimed the freedom of Mexico. He ruled, as Emperor Augustin I, for a short time before he was exiled and executed.

Other rulers came and went. Then in 1829, Spain made a last effort to regain her colony. Four thousand troops were landed at Tampico. They surrendered to López de Santa Anna, who became president and then a despotic dictator.

Texas seceded from Mexico, and Santa Anna personally led a Mexican army against the Texans, but when he was captured in the battle of San Jacinto in 1836, he granted independence to Texas in order to secure his own release.

Again it was Santa Anna who lost all of Mexico's land north of the Rio Grande to the United States following the disastrous war with our country in 1846–48—not a very bright chapter in United States history. But in spite of his mismanagement and despotic rule, Santa Anna continued in power until the people finally rose against him and deposed him permanently in 1855.

Now a truly great leader came from the ranks in the person of Benito Juárez, a full-blood Zapotec Indian, who became a national hero.

JUAREZ AND INDIANS
FROM HIS DISTRICT

Juárez's administration had many battles to fight, first with disgruntled land-owners who did not go along with his land reforms and then with the French and the Mexican liberals who organized a government and invited Archduke Maximilian of Austria as Emperor. Unfortunately for Maximilian, France stopped sending troops for his support when the United States insisted on respect for the Monroe Doctrine.

Emperor Maximilian was captured and shot in 1867.

Five years later Juárez died in office, and for many years the country was in the grip of ruthless and despotic dictators, who ruled by terror and held the working classes in virtual slavery. The Revolution of 1910 was the prophecy of a new day to come, however, which reached fulfillment when General Lázaro Cárdenas became president in 1934. He returned much land to the people, ended foreign exploitation, restored the Church, and built roads, schools, and other public works. The presidents that have followed him have been elected by popular vote and have continued to work for the good of the republic, both nationally and internationally, so that Mexico has been able to take its place in world affairs.

Things to think about

What findings indicate the earliest man came to the New World from Asia?

What important present-day animal, native to the New World, went to Asia by the same route and so was saved from extinction!

What civilization of Mexico is older than that of Central Europe?

Tell of the work of the scholars of this civilization and compare their work with scholars of Greece and Rome of the same date.

How many ancient civilizations can be traced in Mexico?

What barbaric tribe conquered and ruled the Valley of Mexico!

How did the coming of Cortés destroy the Aztec culture?

How many years after the Spanish invaded Mexico did John Smith arrive at Jamestown, Virginia?

What ruler created political and economical turbulence in Mexico from 1812 to 1855? What was the form of government then? What territory was lost to Mexico?

How do the lives of Abraham Lincoln and Benito Juárez compare?

Life in Mexico today

Government

Today the President is elected by the people for one term of six years, and he may never be re-elected. His cabinet, which he appoints, is quite similar to the cabinet of the U.S. President, but there is no vice-president. The Mexican Congress is composed of the Senate and Chamber of Deputies, which is much like the U.S. House of Representatives. Senators are elected for six years and deputies for three, and neither can run for re-election for the following term. The Mexican Supreme Court members are appointed by the President with the approval of the Senate.

The national capital is Mexico City, and it is situated in the Federal District, which corresponds to the District of Columbia in the United States. The government of each state is also much like that of the states in the United States.

Natural Resources

Mexico's rich mineral resources have been used since the days of the Aztecs, whose gold and silver ornaments the Spaniards melted down and shipped, in the form of bricks, to their country across the sea. But far more valuable to the prehistoric Indian were the many wild plants from which he obtained his food, for they were his very life. Even now the inhabitants find many uses for the wild plants that still grow in Mexico.

Much of Mexico is covered with forests, which contain valuable hardwoods and dyewoods, in addition to evergreens and oak. The Mexican government has set aside nearly fifty of these forests as national parks.

A tree which grows in great numbers in the Yucatán jungles should be of interest to children, for it produces the chicle from which chewing gum is made. That is the sapodilla tree, which also bears delicious fruit about the size of an orange. The wood of this tree was favored by the

Mayas for building purposes because it is harder and more lasting even than mahogany. The chicle is a milky sap, which is gathered by the Indians, descendants of the ancient Mayas, much as maple sap is harvested in this country.

Farming and Grazing

Long before Columbus stumbled onto the New World, farming was an important industry in Mexico. By the time of the Aztecs, a wide variety of plants was being cultivated, including corn, squash, pumpkins, beans, tomatoes, red and green peppers, avocados, pineapples, vanilla, cacao, and cotton. Chocolate, made from the cacao bean, was a favorite drink of the Aztecs, and the bean was so highly prized that it was used as money. The Aztecs also made rubber from the guayule plant and a fermented drink, called pulque, from the maguey plant. Pulque, a mild alcoholic drink, is still popular in Mexico.

Sixty per cent of Mexico's population is engaged in agriculture today, and it is the country's most important industry, although much of the land is unfit for cultivation. The amount of land under cultivation is rapidly increasing, however, due to the building of dams and improved methods of irrigation, agricultural research, and other efforts of the government to better the conditions in rural areas.

Until well into this century, most of the land was owned by a few wealthy people and worked by the poorest class, called peons, who were always in debt to the owners and had no land and few belongings of their own. A few large haciendas still exist, but much of the farming land now consists of small tracts, owned by individual farmers, and "ejidos," which are worked communally, a practice that goes back to the Aztecs, when the land was held in common by the community and tracts assigned to families for farming. Torreón is the center of a large irrigated area, called La Laguna, that is communally owned and cooperatively worked. Farming here is carried on by the most advanced methods, but some of the southern Indians still use the ancient Aztec planting stick, while others use the wooden plow, drawn by oxen, that was first introduced by the Spaniards.

Although Mexico lies in the subtropical and tropical zones, farm products are influenced more by altitude than latitude. Corn, the nation's basic food, grows all over Mexico, but the kind produced differs widely with climatic conditions. Wheat and other grains grow in irrigated sections of the Central Plateau and northern uplands. The production of cotton has increased sharply in recent years, and Mexico is now one of the leading cotton countries. Most of it is grown in the irrigated La Laguna area of Durango and Coahuila and in the section around Mexicali in northern Baja California.

Other crops which grow at a moderate altitude are coffee, sugar cane, tobacco, alfalfa, chili peppers, potatoes, beans, and other vegetables. During the winter, such vegetables as tomatoes, peas, and lettuce are grown along the west coast and shipped to the United States. Cotton and sugar cane grow on the hot, humid gulf coastal plain, along with cacao, coconuts, vanilla, citrus fruits, and bananas, pineapples, and other tropical fruits. Yucatán, with its limestone soil, is famous for raising henequén; the fibers of this interesting plant, which belongs to the amaryllis family, are used in making certain kinds of twine, rope, thread, bags, and other products.

Grazing is important in northern Mexico, near the United States border, where the land is too arid for cultivation. Cattle, sheep, hogs, and goats are raised, and the national government is aiding the growth of the livestock industry by bringing in fine cattle and sheep for breeding purposes. Mexico and the United States have twice cooperated in stamping out epidemics of foot-and-mouth disease.

Mining

Mexico leads the world in the production of silver and is close to the top in lead, sulphur, zinc, copper, and gold. Most important to the nation's progress, however, are petroleum, iron, and coal, for these are used largely within the country, to build up its own industries and advance its standard of living. Most of the other metals, including molybdenum, tungsten, mercury, antimony, tin, arsenic, and manganese, are exported, principally to the United States.

Mexico's oil fields, which lie along the gulf coast in Tamaulipas and Veracruz and the Isthmus of Tehuantepéc, were almost entirely foreign owned until 1938, when President Cárdenas expelled foreign oil companies and took over their properties, paying the companies for them. Since that time, the petroleum industry has been operated by a government-owned company called *Petroleos Mexicanos*, familiarly known as PEMEX.

Iron deposits are located in the northern part of the Sierra Madre Occidental and the northern section of the Central Plateau. The Cerro de Mercado Mine, in the state of Durango, is almost pure iron. The production of coal, as yet, is not sufficient to take care of the nation's needs, and coke is imported in large quantities. Most of the coal fields are situated in north-central Mexico, but a large field has recently been discovered in the state of Oaxaca.

Manufacturing and Industry

On the whole, Mexico's industries are much like those in the United States; in fact, some of the plants are branches of United States companies. But the exquisite native handicraft items that appear in shops and market-places everywhere are peculiarly Mexican. From the days when the Mayan and Toltec and Aztec artisans wove cotton cloth as fine as any silk and made dazzling jewelry from gold and silver and jade and turquoise for the adornment of the nobles and priests, the workers of Mexico have taken great pride in their handiwork and made it truly their own. The lovely products of the silversmiths and tinsmiths, the hand-wrought jewelry, gay serapes, colorful native costumes and fine needlework, the decorative tiles and lacquered trays and bowls, and the ceramics and blown glass in blue, green, amber, and amethyst—all of these are highly prized by tourists and residents alike because of their fine workmanship.

The industrial growth of Mexico has been dramatically advanced by the thousands of miles of new roads and the improved means of transportation and by the new hydroelectric plants that are furnishing power to factories and mills. The nation's supply of electrical power has gone up five hundred per cent in the last few years, and Mexico now leads Latin America in industry. Monterrey has become known as the Mexican Pittsburgh because of its great iron and steel works, but it also has cement works, furniture and glass factories, flour and cotton mills, and many others.

Although the heaviest concentration of industry is in the area of Mexico City, there are industrial plants in almost every part of the nation. The biggest center for the manufacture of textiles is at Puebla, but this industry and related ones are important in at least twenty-five

other cities, as widespread as Nuevo Laredo, Mazatlán, Querétaro, Saltillo, Orizaba, and Guadalajara, which is also famous for its ceramics and beautiful blown glass.

There are smelters and foundries in most of the principal cities and mining centers in northern and central Mexico, including Torreón, Piedras Negras, Chihuahua, and Durango. Oil refineries are in cities near the gulf-coast oil fields, such as Veracruz and Tampico, which are also the country's leading ports. Rope, binding twine, and other products made from henequén are important manufactures in the chief cities of the Yucatán Peninsula. Food processing plants of one kind or another are found in nearly every part of Mexico.

Transportation and Communication

Transportation has always been a difficult problem in Mexico because of the country's extremely mountainous surface, and some areas have scarcely been penetrated as yet. There are, for instance, Indian tribes living in remote mountain valleys in the Chiapas Highlands who cannot speak Spanish, the national language, and who, in fact, have never even heard of Spain and its conquest of the New World.

However, in the last few decades the Mexican government has made remarkable progress in its road-building program, designed to reach as

many of these outlying villages as possible and to open up more areas to agricultural and industrial development. An outstanding result of this program is the new Gulf Highway, which extends from Veracruz to Puerto Juárez, on the Caribbean Coast and, with its auxiliary roads, opens up the Yucatán Peninsula for the first time to automobile and truck travel. Another fine road is the Inter-Ocean Highway, which connects Matamoros, on the gulf coast, with Mazatlán, on the Pacific Coast, by way of the important cities of Monterrey, Saltillo, Torreón, and Durango.

In 1936 there were only 1,500 miles of surfaced roads—paved or graveled—and only one highway that connected Mexico with the United States. This was the Pan-American Highway, which enters Mexico at the border city of Nuevo Laredo. There are now more than 18,000 miles of surfaced roads and many thousands of miles of other roads that form a network over most of the country. The work of building new roads and improving the old ones goes on continually.

In addition to the Pan-American Highway, three other paved highways now run between Mexico City and the United States border. The Central Highway, starting at Ciudád Juárez, was opened in 1950, followed in 1952 by the Pacific Highway, from Nogales. The newest highway starts at Piedras Negras and is sometimes called the Constitution Highway because it was opened to travel in 1957, the centennial of the signing of Mexico's constitution in 1857; the road has been given the number 57 for the same reason.

The Pan-American Highway has long been a project of all the Americas. The world's longest highway, it starts at Fairbanks, Alaska, and goes through nineteen countries to Rio de Janeiro and other points in South America. More than 4,000 miles of it are in Mexico. Most of the road is passable now in good weather, but much of it is not yet paved.

The network of railroads, while not as widespread as that of the highways, connects the more densely populated areas with each other, with outlying areas, and with ports on both coasts. Branch railways extend into some of the more remote agricultural and industrial sections, and feeder highways from railroad points are opening up other areas. Mexico City is the most important rail center, but railroad lines also go out in all directions from Monterrey and San Luis Potosí.

The National Railways, owned by the Federal Government, is the largest system. Centered at Mexico City, its lines go north to the United States border and south to Guatemala, as well as to many points in Mexico. The Pacific Railroad, which is also owned by the Federal Government, parallels the Pacific Highway from Nogales to Guadalajara. The Tehuantepéc Railroad crosses the Isthmus of Tehuantepéc, and the United Railways of Yucatán serve the henequén plantations. The Southeastern Railway, which was built some years before the Gulf Highway, opened a land route between the Yucatán Peninsula and the rest of Mexico for the first time in the nation's history.

Commercial aviation has been important in Mexico since 1917, when Mexico City became the first capital city on the North American Continent to have airmail service. The nation is served by three Mexican air lines, and numerous air lines from the United States and other countries fly into Mexico City.

Mexico was the first Latin-American nation to have television, and the country also has several hundred radio stations. The nation has radiotelephone and radiotelegraph connections with most of the world and is constantly working to improve its internal telephone and telegraph networks. In 1949 the Federal Government took over all international telegraph facilities from three United States companies.

The People

About ten per cent of Mexico's thirty-five million people are white, mostly Spanish; fifteen per cent are pure Indian, consisting of more than fifty groups, each with its own language; and seventy-five per cent are the mestizos, a blend, in varying degrees, of white and Indian. The largest concentration of population is on the temperate Central Plateau, particularly in the Valley of Mexico, where Mexico City and its environs have about five million inhabitants.

Until recently, the population has been seventy-five per cent rural, but, of late years, there has been a movement to the cities, especially among the landless members of the lower class, of which there is still a considerable number. There is also a movement to the newly irrigated areas in the north, which the government is making available to the people as rapidly as possible. In the cities, the worst of the slums are being replaced by modern housing developments, and the picturesque open markets are giving way to new, more hygienic supermarkets.

The Mexicans are a gentle, courteous, and deeply religious people, and, for the most part, a happy people, despite the poverty that prevails among the lower class, constituting about sixty-five per cent of the population. Although life is often hard for them, they have great pride in their country and in their democratic government, which is attempting to insure them health, education, and security. This is not an easy undertaking when one considers the large number of different Indian tribes in the southern and western mountains, each with its own language.

A love for beauty and art and dancing and music is a part of the people's heritage, not only from Spain but from the ancient Indian civilizations. The dooryard of the humblest hut is apt to be graced with lovely flowers and the interior with some sort of adornment, however small. The huts, usually one or two rooms, are clean, and so are the children, for Mexicans, however poor, have a strong sense of personal cleanliness.

Music is everywhere, and a fiesta is held at the slightest excuse, when the people sing and dance and wear their gay native costumes. Market-day, too, is a colorful occasion, when Indians in native dress come from outlying villages to sell their produce and items of handicraft.

The Zinacantecos, descendants of the Mayas living in Chiapas, are distinguished by their flat straw hats with bright-colored ribbon streamers and their pink-striped serapes. The Chamulas wear white sombreros and knee-length fringed tunics. The Tehuanan women, on the Isthmus of Tehuantepéc, are famous for their handsome, embroidered dresses with long, full skirts that end in wide white ruffles. On special days, they wear elaborate headdresses of pleated starched lace, called *huipiles*. According to tradition, the custom originated when a shipload of baby dresses was wrecked off the coast, and the women, not knowing what they were for, wore them as headdresses.

Many Indians proudly calling themselves Aztecs still live in central Mexico, and many Mayas live near the ancient Mayan ruins on the Yucatán Peninsula, comprising about half of the population on the peninsula. In the state of Oaxaca, the Zapotec and Mixtec Indians, living near the ruins of Monte Albán and Mitla, their ancestral homes, have given several famous leaders to Mexico.

The lives of the Indians today often reflect customs and practices of their ancestors. In many villages women must still carry the water for household use from the village well to their homes, and grind the corn for their tortillas with the same kind of grinding stone, or "metate," that was used by their ancestors hundreds of years ago. The men still plant their corn with sharp-pointed sticks and carry their produce to market on their backs, anchored by means of templines—a sort of strap—fastened around their foreheads.

Most of the Mexicans are devout Catholics. Their religious holidays are occasions for elaborate processions. The joyous feast days are celebrated as festivals, with native music, colorful costumes, feasting and dancing.

The Arts

Antonio de Mendoza was named the first Viceroy of New Spain (Mexico) in 1535 and ruled until 1550 when he was sent as Viceroy to Peru and was replaced by Luís de Velasco. Mexico made its greatest progress in the first half century of its existence. The printing press was introduced in 1536; the great artists of Spain came to Mexico to adorn its cathedrals; extensive explorations were made; and maritime relations with the Philippines were established.

A flowering of the literary arts began in the 17th century, and Mexico produced men and women of letters and science such as Juana de la Crúz; Juan Ruíz de Alarcón; the historian, Javier de Clavijero; the astronomer, Siguenza y Góngora; the geographer, José Antonio Alzate y Ramirez; and the encyclopedist, Antonio de Leon y Gama.

Influenced by the rich heritage of the ancient Indian civilizations,

Mexican architects blend the best of Europe and America with a color and flair that belong only to Mexico. Nowhere else will you find such a mixture of handsome old European cathedrals and palaces, decorated with the goldwork that is characteristic of the Aztecs and their descendants; the old Spanish houses with their inner courtyards and gardens; and the ultra-modern glass and steel hotels, skyscrapers, and other buildings, decorated with typically Mexican murals, mosaics, and sculpture on every available surface.

Mexico City is a good place to find practically all of Mexico's different kinds of architecture. A fine example of the colonial baroque style, which was popular in the sixteenth to eighteenth centuries, is the cathedral on the north side of the Zócalo, the city's central square. Erected on the site of the great temple to the Aztec god of war, this cathedral was begun in 1573 and replaced the first church on the North American continent, which was built on the same site by Cortés in 1525.

Many of the buildings of University City, new site of the National University of Mexico, are good examples of modern architecture decorated with Indian motifs. The rectangular, box-like library building, ten stories high, is covered with a striking and intricate mosaic of stone. It was done by the famous artist Juan O'Gorman and tells the story of Mexican culture before and after the Spanish conquest. Other University buildings and government buildings in Mexico City and elsewhere are decorated with the murals of such great artists as Diego Rivera, José Clemente Orozco, David Alfaro Siqueiros, and Rufino Tamayo, and the murals and pictorial maps of Miguel Covarrubias, who was a noted author as well as artist. A new style of modern architecture, called "shell," which was developed by Mexican architects Félix Candela and Enrique de la Mora, is represented in University City by the little Cosmic Ray Pavilion.

Architects and builders have a special problem in Mexico City, because the city is built on an ancient lake bed and the heavy buildings sink deeper and deeper into the spongy soil. Modern architects have been quite ingenious in meeting this problem, but older buildings have sunk six feet or more, and great cracks in the walls of the cathedral have had to be repaired.

Old Spanish homes are generally in the older sections of the city, such as the suburb of Coyoacán, whose high walls and narrow, cobblestone streets are in sharp contrast to its two modern "shell" churches—the little Chapel of the Missionaries of the Holy Ghost and the Chapel of the Sisters of Charity of St. Vincent de Paul. The newest and most unconventional residences are in the Jardines del Pedregal, once a lava-field "badlands" shunned by the natives. Now the newly-rich build modernistic homes there and use the lava rock for making walls and steps and fish ponds and swimming pools.

Music and dancing are almost as important to the average Mexican as eating and sleeping, as is evidenced by the frequent fiestas. Strolling musicians, marimba bands, even organ grinders are encouraged to make music on city streets, in the parks, and in the public markets. They sing and play Mexico's own special brand of popular tunes or a combination of Spanish and Indian folk music, of which the nation has a rich heritage. In Mexico City, Mexico folklore ballets are presented in the Folklore Center.

Probably the best-known composer is Carlos Chavez, who has been director of several music institutions in the nation, including the Symphony Orchestra of Mexico. In his own compositions, Chavez has made use of the folk music and legends of the ancient Indian civilizations, as well as those of present-day Indians. His ballets, *The Four Suns* and *New Fire*, tell the story, in music, of ancient Indian legends, and his *Xochipili-Macuilxochitl* attempts to re-create a pre-Columbian orchestra. Chavez' ballet-symphony, *H.P.*, had its premiere in the United States.

Drama, some of which is sponsored by the government, is also highly rated, and outdoor and classical productions are especially well attended. People flock to the pyramid of Teopanzolco, at Cuernavaca, to see *The Return of Quetzalcoatl*, an open-air presentation of Aztec legends, rituals, music, and dancing. Even more thousands attend the classical Spanish plays put on by the inhabitants of Guanajuato, who use the narrow, picturesque streets and the plazas, fountains, and balconies of their sixteenth-century town as stage settings.

Literature started in Mexico with the chronicles of the conquistadors

NATIONAL UNIVERSITY,
MEXICO CITY

—notably, those of Hernán Cortés and Bernal Diaz del Castillo—and the religious writings of the missionaries. The first book to be printed in the Western Hemisphere was published in Mexico City in 1539. Sister Juana Inés de la Cruz was a famous nun-poet of the seventeenth century.

José Joaquin Fernandez de Lizardi, who lived from 1776 to 1827, was a champion of independence. He founded a revolutionary journal and wrote the satirical novel, *The Itching Parrot*, which was the first novel written by a native of Spanish America. Novelists who have written about the Revolution of 1910 are Martin Luis Guzman, who wrote *The Eagle and the Serpent*, and Mariano Azuela, author of *The Underdogs*. Noted present-day poets are Alfonso Reyes, who is also an essayist and literary critic of distinction, and Jaime Torres Bodet, versatile and distinguished Secretary of Public Education. From 1948 to 1952, Dr. Bodet served as Director General of UNESCO (the United Nations Educational, Scientific, and Cultural Organization).

Education

Mexico's advance in education has been the most amazing of all the reforms the government has been carrying on. Time was when a large percentage of the population could neither read nor write, and "evangelistas," or public scribes, in almost every plaza made a good living writing letters for those who could not do it for themselves. Now the spread of public education has just about put the evangelistas out of business. This has resulted partly from a unique educational program begun in 1944 when the President issued a decree that every literate person—that is, every person who could read and write—from the fifth grade up, must teach at least one illiterate person to read and write, or pay someone else to do so. Many public and private organizations are helping with the program, and the Department of Public Education has furnished specially written primers, some of them in native Indian languages, since many Indians do not speak Spanish.

To meet the goal of public education for every child, thousands of prefabricated schools are going up all over the country. These are paid for by the government and installed by the people of each community, for Mexicans very much want education for their children and themselves. Teachers for the schools are being trained in more than seventy normal schools, and millions of free textbooks are being distributed.

To further its educational campaign, the government is sending cultural missions and mobile medical units, where possible, into the more backward communities and Indian villages, to teach not only reading and writing and the Spanish language, but a better way of life, as well. Some of this is done with puppet shows, which the Indians flock to see.

Mexico has many colleges, universities, and technical schools, most famous of which is the National University, founded in Mexico City in 1551 as the Royal and Pontifical University of Mexico. It now occupies a beautiful new campus of more than eighty buildings, called University City, and has an attendance of 70,000 students, from all over the world.

MURAL, NATIONAL UNIVERSITY

Things to think about

What influences Mexico's wide, wide range of growing things?

Tell how recently-built government roads are reaching isolated tribes in Mexico who know nothing of the Spanish conquests.

How have the ancient cultures of Mexico influenced present-day artists?

Tell how Mexico, with the oldest colleges and universities in the New World, faced a badly needed reform in education as late as 1944.

TAXCO

The enchantment of Mexico

Enchantment at Every Turn

Nowhere else in America will you find the special kind of enchantment that is Mexico—its scenery, its prehistoric ruins, its centuries-old churches and cathedrals, its colonial towns and Indian villages and market places, its fiestas, and, above all, its people.

The scenery of this fascinating country ranges from hot, arid deserts, with many kinds of cactus, yuccas and other desert plants, to rugged mountain ranges and lush, green jungles, filled with exotic tropical plants and alive with parrots and other brightly colored birds. Much of the wilderness area, especially in the Sierra Madres, is still unexplored, but the thousands of miles of roads that have been built in recent years have given access to some magnificent scenery.

The road from Mexico City to Veracruz goes through miles of mountainous and desert country before it leaves the tableland and drops 3,000 feet through subtropical forests, orchards, and coffee plantations to Orizaba. Throughout the descent, the towering, snow-capped Orizaba Volcano is in view. Beyond Orizaba is lovely Fortín de las Flores, famous for its bougainvilleas, camellias, orchids, azaleas, and other tropical and subtropical flowers. A hotel in the town has a swimming pool blanketed with floating gardenias. A second road to Veracruz branches off twenty-five miles east of Puebla and passes the extinct volcano Cofre de Perote, before it drops down into tropical Jalapa Valley. The old Spanish town of Jalapa also has a profusion of flowers, as well as narrow cobblestone streets and white colonial houses with roofs of red tile.

The road from Matamoros southwest across the nation to Mazatlán via Torreón, follows a highly scenic route, and so does much of the Pacific Highway. South of Guadalajara, the Pacific Highway borders Lake Chapala and passes through several Indian fishing villages on the lake shore. Farther on, the Paricutín Volcano can be reached on a very rough road from Uruapan, 45 miles south of the highway. Lake Pátzcuaro, also on the Pacific Highway, is famous for the "butterfly" nets which the Tarascan Indians use to fish its waters. There are numerous Indian fishing villages around the shore and one on an island in the lake.

East of Morelia the road reaches its highest point, 9,469 feet, and a few miles farther, at Mil Cumbres in Atzimba National Park, there is a splendid view of range upon range of high mountain peaks.

Wildlife

Mexico's wildlife includes such unusual animals as the cacomistle and the coatimundi, the jaguar, the jaguarundi, and the ocelot. The cacomistle, also called ringtail, is known for its long, bushy tail, ringed by alternating bands of black and white. A cousin of the raccoon, this little animal, which is about the size of a house cat and an even better mouser, can leap through the trees like a squirrel. The coatimundi, or coati, also somewhat resembles the raccoon, but it has a long, slender tail and a long, upturned snout. The coatimundis are gregarious and often travel in bands of from ten to twenty, sometimes with their tails stuck straight up in the air. They are friendly creatures and make good pets.

The jaguarundi belongs to the cat family, but it looks more like an otter and, unlike most cats, enjoys swimming. In Mexico, it is often called "otter-cat." It is larger than an ordinary cat, weighing from ten to twenty pounds. The ocelot, a sleek, handsomely spotted cat, weighs 25 to 35 pounds. Its first cousin, the margay, is smaller but has a much longer tail. Largest of all the North American cats is the strong, fierce jaguar, who was worshipped as a god by the ancient Indians and is greatly feared by the present natives of Mexico; they call him *el tigre*.

Many of these animals have found their way across the border into Texas and the Southwest, but they are not common in the United States. The Mexican nine-banded armadillo has wandered as far north as Kansas and as far east as Florida. This strange little animal, with his "suit of armor," has southern relatives that range in size from five inches to five feet. Another animal that often crosses the border is the peccary or javelina, a small wild pig which travels in herds and, when startled, emits a strong odor from musk glands in his back.

The Gulf of California is famous as the winter breeding ground of a huge herd of gray whales, which migrate from there to the Bering Sea. These animals almost became extinct, but are now protected from whalers, and are making a good comeback. Another animal which almost died out before it was afforded protection is the enormous sea elephant, or elephant seal. These exceedingly homely, but interesting, animals are found in fairly large numbers on Guadalupe, San Benito, and other Mexican islands off the coast of Lower California.

Prehistoric Indian Ruins

Many of the prehistoric ruins have been excavated and restored and are open to public viewing. Many more still lie buried beneath the accumulation of the ages.

One of the most important restorations is at Yucatán's ruined Mayan city of Chichén Itzá. About 75 miles easy of Mérida, the ruins are reached by the new Gulf Highway. A branch road goes to the ruins of Uxmál, about fifty miles south of Mérida. One of the largest structures at Chichén Itzá is the Castillo, which is not a castle at all, but a huge pyramid, topped by the temple of the god Kukulcán, whose symbolic feathered-serpent columns guard the doorways. Feathered serpents also guard the Temple of Warriors, a huge building flanked by numerous columns that may have supported the roof of a public market. A round "observatory" was named the Caracol by the Spanish because of its circular staircase, which ascends to a small room with thick walls containing long, narrow openings. These were probably used by the priests for observing the movements of the sun, moon, and stars.

CHICHEN ITZA

PATIO DE LAS
MONJAS, UXMAL

Another interesting building is the Ball Court, with its stone rings on the walls high above the court floor. This court was used for an exciting Mayan ball game, in which the players attempted to put a ball through the ring by hitting it with some part of their bodies other than their hands, which they were not permitted to use.

Scientists, with the aid of divers and air pumps, are recovering thousands of treasures thrown into the Sacred Cenote as offerings to the gods.

Outstanding buildings at Uxmál include the Nunnery, the Governor's Palace, and the House of the Pigeons, so called because the many openings in its walls resemble a huge dovecot. At Palenque, a Mayan city that is even older than Uxmál and Chichén Itzá, are the lovely Temple of the Sun, decorated with stucco friezes, and the elaborate structure named El Palacio by the Spaniards, who thought it was a palace.

The Temple of Niches still stands at Tajín, near Papantla, Veracruz, and the Totonac Indians hold their Flying Pole Dance, or Dance of the Voladores, in front of it. The white buildings of Monte Albán and Mitla's rectangular, intricately carved palaces, near Oaxaca, have been restored. Both of these cities are believed to have been built by prehistoric Zapotec Indians and then abandoned to the Mixtecs.

Cholula, near Puebla, contains the highest pyramid in Mexico. This was once the Toltec sacred city of Quetzalcoatl, but the Spanish destroyed the city's many temples and built churches on their sites, so that now the countryside is dotted with churches of the Spanish colonial period. Southwest of Cuernavaca, the Pyramid of Xochicalco is one of the most beautiful in Mexico. Hieroglyphics and Indian motifs on other ruins which are being excavated in the vicinity indicate that Xochicalco may have been a crossroads for Indians from all over Mexico.

In the outskirts of Mexico City is the Aztec Pyramid of Tenayuca, which was the base for twin temples dedicated to the god of agriculture and the god of war. A few miles farther north are the ruins of Teotihuacán, "Abode of the Gods."

ABODE OF THE GODS

Cities and Towns

Handsome public buildings, cobblestone streets and old colonial homes, colorful public markets thronged with gay crowds, street music, flowers, fiestas—these are a few of the things that add to the enchantment of the cities and towns and villages.

MEXICO CITY

Mexico City, with its many contrasts, is about as enchanting a place as one could hope to find. Built on the old Aztec central plaza, the Plaza de la Constitución, better known as the Zócalo, is the heart of the city. On one side, where a great Aztec temple once stood, is the handsome Cathedral of Mexico. On the site of Montezuma's Palace the National Palace now stands, originally built by Cortés for his home.

Many changes have been made in it since then, and it now contains the offices of the President, the Treasury, and several other national departments.

Many other historic and interesting buildings are in the vicinity of the Zócalo. The National Museum of Anthropology, home of the Aztec Calendar Stone, contains a wealth of other relics of the prehistoric Indian civilizations. The National Institute of Fine Arts, formerly the Academy of San Carlos, houses a valuable collection of early Mexican artists and seventeenth-century European painters. West of the Zócalo, the magnificent Palace of Fine Arts contains auditoriums, art galleries, a ballroom, and the National Theater, where the famous curtain of Tiffany glass, valued at thousands of dollars, is on display.

The city's main avenue, Paseo de la Reforma, which starts at the traffic circle on the Avenida Juárez, ends two miles away at Chapultepec Park. Now lined with the most modern of skyscrapers, as well as with the old Spanish and French buildings, this boulevard was constructed by the Emperor Maximilian to shorten the distance between the National Palace and his summer home in Chapultepec Castle. The traffic circles, which are called *glorietas* and contain monuments and flowers, occur at frequent intervals in the boulevard. The mounted figure of Charles IV of Spain, which stands in the first glorieta, is called "the Little Horse" by the Mexicans.

Montezuma's summer home was on the site of the present castle in Chapultepec Park—"Chapultepec" is Aztec for grasshopper—and Mexican presidents used the castle as a residence for many years. Now it is the National Museum of History, and the park is a favorite Sunday spot for Mexico City residents. In the park are age-old cypresses, or ahuehuete trees, some of which have grown to a very large size. The one named "Tree of Montezuma" is 170 feet high and 50 feet in circumference.

Near the west end of the Paseo is the Rancho del Charro, the field where the elaborately dressed *charros* hold public riding exhibitions. The charro is a "gentleman" horseman, in contrast to the *vaquero*, who is a working cowboy.

The city has many small parks, filled with flowers and laughing

children. It also has the largest bull ring in the world. Some of the famous spots in the suburbs are the Basilica of Guadalupe in the Villa Madero, the 1768 Franciscan convent at Churubúsco, now a museum, and the "floating" gardens of Xochimilco, which no longer float but are anchored by long roots to the bottom of the lake. Picturesque boats make their way along the canals among the gardens.

Northwest of Mexico City is the Bajío, a great, fertile plain that is the cradle of Mexican independence. In the colonial towns on this plain were laid the first plans for the fight for freedom from Spain. One of these, Querétaro, at the junction of the Central Highway and the Constitution Highway, has been important throughout the history of Mexico. In addition to the town's role in the struggle for national independence, the peace treaty between Mexico and the United States was signed here, the Emperor Maximilian was executed here—on the Hill of the Bells—and Fray Junípero Serra set out from here to establish his chain of missions in California. Although Querétaro is rapidly becoming an important industrial center, the town is preserving its fine old colonial buildings, its lovely landscaping, and its remarkable old aqueduct that dates from Spanish occupancy.

San Miguel de Allende was founded as an Otomi Indian mission in 1542 by Fray Juan de San Miguel. The town was named for its founder, but "de Allende" was later added in honor of its native son and revolutionary hero Ignacio José de Allende, who was executed with Father Miguel Hidalgo. San Miguel, once the center for great haciendas, is spread out over rolling green hills. The beautiful old houses, with coats-of-arms carved over the doorways, were built by wealthy Spanish aristocracy. There are numerous old churches in the town and just outside it, and the famous School of Arts and Crafts occupies one of the old convents.

Thirty miles to the north, in the village of Dolores Hidalgo, is the little parish church where Father Hidalgo called his people to fight for freedom. Hidalgo, Mexico's national hero, was born in the village.

Guanajuato, scene of the outdoor drama described earlier, centers a fabulous silver-mining area which has supplied a large portion of the world's silver. Except for Mexico City, Guanajuato was the wealthiest

FLOATING GARDENS, XOCHIMILCO

STREET OF THE KISS, GUANAJUATO

city in the nation during the height of the silver-mining industry.

Set in a deep mountain gorge high above the great plain, the town is reached on a side road which passes through the ruins of the old colonial town of Marfíl. Much of the wealth that was received from the silver mines was spent on the handsome colonial homes and churches that line the narrow, steep streets. One street is so narrow that it is called the Street of the Kiss. Points of historical interest are the *Alhóndiga de Granaditas* (Public Granary), where the revolutionaries killed many Spanish royalists; the Church La Parroquia, containing the image of the Virgin of Guanajuato, brought from Spain in 1557; the Juárez Theater; and the Church of La Valenciana, just outside of town.

Chihuahua, where Father Hidalgo awaited execution, is northern Mexico's most important city. Center of a rich mining and stock-raising area, it is also noted for the tiny hairless Chihuahua dogs that originated there. Historic spots are the tower in which Hidalgo was imprisoned, the eighteenth-century cathedral, and the home of Pancho Villa, Mexican bandit and revolutionary.

Cuernavaca, on the road to Acapulco, contains one of the oldest churches in America, a fine old Franciscan cathedral. Founded in 1521 on the site of an Aztec community, it was one of thirty cities given to Cortés by the Spanish king. Cortés' palace has been restored and houses the offices of the state legislature. Diego Rivera painted a series of murals on the walls as a gift to the Mexican people from Dwight Morrow, the late United States Ambassador to Mexico.

About fifty miles farther south is Taxco, one of the most interesting and famous towns in Mexico. An old Aztec town on the side of a steep mountain, it was conquered by the Spanish in 1531. A Frenchman, Joseph le Borde, discovered a rich vein of ore near the town and, in gratitude, built the beautiful Santa Prisca Church and richly ornamented it. In order to preserve the town's colonial charm, the government has made Taxco a national monument and will not allow anything to be changed or any modern buildings to be erected. Mexico's best silverwork is done in the workrooms of Taxco and sold in its shops and colorful Sunday market.

Acapulco, glamorous favorite of wealthy American tourists, encircles a turquoise bay on the Pacific Coast. The cliffs that rise behind the city are studded with luxury hotels and expensive villas, and white beaches fringe the shore. Yachts and aquaplanes have replaced the sailing ships, loaded with silks and spices, that once crowded the harbor, for Acapulco, founded in 1550, is the oldest port on the North American Pacific Coast. The Castillo San Diego, at the entrance to the harbor, was built to guard the port from pirates.

Guadalajara, on the Pacific Highway, is Mexico's second-largest city and a thriving commercial center, but it has none of the bustle of the nation's capital. Instead, an air of tranquility and happiness dominates the city, which was founded as the City of the Holy Ghost in 1530. The lovely old colonial buildings, open-air patios, flower-filled parks and plazas, and pleasant climate add to its charm. The city is the birthplace of the famous artist José Clemente Orozco, and it displays many of his murals. Many of Mexico's popular songs and dances also originated here, including the picturesque *jarabe tapatio*, or Hat Dance. Points of interest are the University, the Cathedral and other colonial churches, the State Museum, the *Hospicio*, the Government Palace, and the Degollado Theater.

Several Indian villages, famous for their pottery, are near Guadalajara, and so is the 2,000-foot deep Oblatos Gorge. The magnificent Juanacatlán Falls, second highest on the continent, are between the city and Lake Chapala.

The Pan-American Highway between Mexico City and Guatemala is known as the Christopher Columbus Highway, and there are numerous interesting towns and villages and beautiful scenery along it. Oaxaca, in the subtropical Oaxaca Valley, is the center of the Zapotec and Mixtec Indian country, and the ruins of Monte Albán and Mitla are nearby. The handsome colonial homes and churches are mostly built of the native green marble, with elaborate wrought-iron trim. Saturday is market day, when the Indians, in their native dress, come in from the surrounding countryside to sell their farm produce and their exquisite handicraft. Near Oaxaca, at Santa Maria del Tule, is the huge old ahuehuete tree called the Tule Tree, possibly the oldest living tree in the world.

Farther south, on the Isthmus of Tehuantepéc, are the two enchanting villages of Tehuantepec and Juchitán, where the Tehuana women are famous for their beautifully embroidered dresses and gold jewelry. San Cristóbal las Casas, oldest Spanish town in the state of Chiapas, has narrow, winding streets, houses with grilled windows, and ornate churches. Its market is thronged with Indians in native costume, whose villages can be reached only afoot or on horseback.

Veracruz, important port and rapidly expanding industrial center, is a curious blend of the old and the new. The city was founded in 1519 when Cortés landed on the gulf coast, and many a ship, bound for Cuba or Spain, was loaded in its harbor with treasure plundered from the Aztecs. United States troops occupied the city in 1847, and the French took it in 1862, in the invasion that installed Maximilian as emperor. Before that, there was a constant threat from pirates, and the old fortress, San Juan de Ulúa, on an island in the harbor, bears many scars. The narrow streets and old colonial houses are in strange contrast to the bustling activity, the modern factories, and the bathing beaches and boat clubs.

VERACRUZ

Fiestas

It's always fiesta time somewhere in Mexico. The ability to hold a fiesta at the drop of a hat is characteristic of Mexicans. Each little town and village has its own patron saint, and there are various other holy days to be celebrated as well. There are also many civic holidays, most of which are celebrated all over the nation.

The religious holidays begin with solemn High Mass, usually followed by dancing and gayety. Sometimes these dances are native ones, once danced in honor of pagan gods long before Christianity was brought to the New World. Sometimes they are dances that were brought from Spain in colonial times, but have now been so changed by the Indians that the priests who introduced them to New Spain would have a hard time recognizing them.

Rodeos, bullfighting, social dancing, feasting, and fireworks are also a part of the fiesta. A popular fireworks display is the *castillo*, which is a complicated structure of fireworks, often thirty feet high; the fireworks set each other off in sequence, resulting in a magnificent and dramatic

display. After the fireworks, the Indians wrap their serapes around them and sleep on the hard ground until daylight, when they return to their villages.

Independence Days, September 15–16, are important national civic holidays, for they celebrate the call to freedom uttered by Father Hidalgo in 1810. Important events are the shouting of the *grito* and the tolling of bells, followed by the usual fireworks, and the military parade at noon the next day. Another important national holiday, on May 5, commemorates the victory of the Mexican army over the French forces at Puebla in 1862. This also is celebrated with military parades and, in some towns, the Battle of Puebla is re-enacted, with the funeral procession and burial of the dead at nightfall.

Some of the national civic holidays are Constitution Day, February 5, which honors both the 1857 constitution and the 1917 one, which was an outgrowth of the Revolution of 1910; the Birthday of Benito Juárez, on March 21; Labor Day, May 1; and Columbus Day, October 12. This is called *Dia de la Raza*—Day of the Race—in Mexico, because the discovery of America by Columbus resulted in the fusion of Spanish and Indian blood to make a new race—the mestizo. The anniversary of the Revolution of 1910 is celebrated by Mexico on November 20.

Some of the important and interesting religious holidays are the Day of Our Lady of Guadalupe, on December 12; the Christmas season, from December 16 to 24 (really to January 6); and Holy Week, beginning with Palm Sunday. December 12 is one of the biggest days in the life of the Mexicans. According to legend, on this day in 1531 the Virgin of Guadalupe first appeared to a lowly Indian, named Juan Diego. Following her instructions, he gathered roses on a barren hillside where only cactus had grown; and when he opened his mantle to show the roses to the Bishop, a picture of the Virgin was impressed on it.

Guadalupe Day is celebrated all over Mexico, for every town has its Guadalupe Church. Celebrations start a week ahead and end with a grand climax on December 12. The most famous Guadalupe Church is the Basilica in Villa Madero, in the outskirts of Mexico City. Thousands throng to the celebration at this church, some of them traveling for a week or more on foot or on burros. Many of the worshipers approach the shrine on their knees. The celebrants sleep in the streets or on the plaza and shop at the many stands set up for their convenience. *Conchero* dancers are an interesting part of the festivities. These are groups of dancers who go from fiesta to fiesta all over the country and dance and play their instruments made from armadillo shells.

During the Christmas season, there is a representation of the Manger of Bethlehem in every home. Some are elaborate and some are simple, but all contain the figures of the Holy Family, the Three Wise Men, the shepherds, the animals, and the Star of Bethlehem. *Posadas*, which are family parties portraying the journey of the Holy Family to Bethlehem, are held nightly. A procession of "pilgrims" goes to the door of a house, knocks, and sings an old song asking for *posada*, or shelter for the night. Voices from within at first refuse, also in song, but when the "pilgrims" reply that it is Mary who asks admittance, the door is flung open and everyone enters for an evening of fun, which centers around a *pinata*.

A *piñata* is a fragile earthenware jar covered with papier-mâché, often in the form of an animal, that is filled with trinkets and sweetmeats. A blindfolded child who has been whirled around and around tries to break the jar with a stick, while the others try to keep the jar out of his reach. Finally, usually after several children have tried, someone gets a good whack at the jar, and there is a grand scramble as everyone tries to get some of the contents that come spilling down. On Christmas Eve, which is known as *Noche Buena*, the Good Night, everyone goes to midnight Mass.

The Christmas season does not end with Christmas Day, but continues through New Year, with its fairs and fireworks, to the Day of the Three Wise Men, on January 6. The children dress up on this day, and many of them set out their shoes to be filled with presents by the Wise Men. Everywhere fancy candies and cakes are for sale.

Another interesting day in January is the 17th, saint day of San Antonio de Padua, patron saint of domestic animals. On this day families decorate their pets with garlands of flowers and take them to church to be blessed by the priest.

Holy Week begins on Palm Sunday with the blessing of the palms. On Maundy Thursday and Good Friday, outdoor passion plays are performed in many towns and villages by the townsfolk themselves. On Saturday is Judas Day, which all Mexican children look forward to. All the preceding week, papier-mâché images of Judas, ranging in size from ten inches to ten feet, with gunpowder in them, have been on sale in the markets and streets. These are hung from balconies and street lights and anywhere else that a place can be found for them. At ten o'clock on Saturday morning, the images are set afire, and the towns are

filled with the noise of their explosions. To add to the din, all the church bells are rung, and the children shake wooden rattles called *matracas*.

The week preceding Lent is carnival time, when everyone stops work and has a good time. Rodeos, balls, and dazzling fireworks are the order of the day. In the village of Huejotzingo, on the road between Mexico City and Puebla, several hundred inhabitants don the costumes of bandits and soldiers and stage a three-day drama, with the entire village as the setting. The story concerns the romance between a sort of Mexican Robin Hood and a girl, acted by a young man in skirts and felt hat, who performs various startling feats. As the story unfolds, the spectators follow the actors through the streets of the town. In addition to the play, there are native dances and a colorful fair.

November 1 is dedicated to all saints, known and unknown. November 2 is All Souls' Day, called in Mexico the *Day of the Dead*. This is not celebrated as a day of mourning but as one of friendliness and good nature. The round loaves of Dead Men's bread produced by the bakeries are relished by the living. Children enjoy the candy skulls that appear in every store and market. Picnics are held in the cemeteries, where the graves are decorated with the yellow calendulas that the Indians believe bring cheer to the dead. On the island of Janitzio, in Lake Pátzcuaro, thousands of candles and garlands of fruit and flowers turn the Tarascan Indian graveyard into fairyland, as the strange Tarascan music swells out over the water.

Another interesting festival of the Tarascan people takes place on February 1 to 8 in the village of Tzintzuntzan on the shore of Lake Pátzcuaro. This includes native dances, an Indian regatta on the lake, and a fair. The humorous *Dance of the Viejitos*, or "Dance of the Little Old Men," is done by very agile young men who are made up to look like wrinkled old men, bent over with age. Tzintzuntzan means *Place of the Humming Birds*, and in pre-Columbian days was the capital city of the Tarascan Indian nation.

These are only a few of the fiestas and dances and customs that reach back to the rich heritage of the Indians and show why the past is so important in the life of Mexico today.

DANCE OF THE
VIEGITOS
(OLD MEN)

Things to think about

What traits have made Mexico a country of gaiety and enchantment?

Tell of some of the fiestas celebrated and the occasions for them.

Why is the birthday of Columbus called "Day of the Race"?

How is the ancient culture of the Indian kept alive by the mestizos in their celebrations?

Pronunciation of Spanish Words

Certain letters in Spanish Words have different sounds from the English letters.

"j" always sounds like "h"
Say Juárez — HWA-ras
Say Baja — Ba-HAH
"h" is always silent
Say hacienda — ah-the-YEHN-dah
"ll" is pronounced "l'y"
Say llama — l'YAH-ma
"n" sounds like "n'y"
"z" sounds like "ss" or "th"
Say Chichén Itzá — Chee-chan-EET-sah

Some dates in Mexican history

1325 Aztec city of Tenochtitlán founded
1519 Cortés landed on gulf coast (Veracruz)
1521 Cortés conquered the Aztecs and founded Mexico on the ruins of their capital
1551 National University founded at Mexico City
1810 Father Miguel Hidalgo summons his people to fight for independence
1821 Independence from Spain attained
1857 Constitution adopted which remained in effect until 1917
1858 Benito Juárez became president for the first time
1864 Maximilian of Austria entered Mexico as Emperor
1867 Maximilian executed by Juárez
1910 Revolution led by Francisco Madero
1917 New Constitution adopted, based on principles of the 1857 one
1934 General Lázaro Cárdenas elected president
1938 Cárdenas expropriated the oil fields

BUTTERFLY NETS,
PATZUCUARO

To the Teacher

The "Enchantment of America" books combine history and geography in a fresh, colorful, and exciting story of the people who have come to the land and of the uses they have made of it.

This book may be read individually for pleasure; or it may be used to enrich a classroom social studies program on Mexico.

Suggested Group Projects

Activities to further acquaint children with the land, the people, and the enchantment of Mexico.

Build a table-top relief map showing the coastal plains, mountains, and central plateau of Mexico.

Have some fun working problems using Mayan number symbols.

Let the paintings on the buildings of the National University inspire the making of a colored-chalk mural.

Have a craft show of Mexican ceramics, basketry, tinware, jewelry, fabrics, glass. Most homes have some interesting pieces of Mexican handiwork.

Model in clay some of the early Mexican artifacts shown on the endsheets of this book.

Make a large, flat, decorative wall map.

Divide a class into two groups; one to research and report on Mayan civilization; and one to report on the Aztecs.

Have a Mexican fiesta.

Index

FLUTED VASE WITH PARROT EFFIGY LEGS, COLIMA
WARRIOR HEAD "HACHA" FORM OF VOLCANIC ROCK, CENTRAL VERACRUZ
CLASSIC SEATED ANIMAL, VOLCANIC ROCK. VERACRUZ
SEATED WARRIOR, JALISCO HOLLOW PAINTED CLAY
CLAY URN ZAPOTECAN FROM OAXACA
PAINTED CLAY WHISTLE SEATED PRIESTESS, ISLAND OF JAINA
HOLLOW PAINTED CLAY WHISTLE, SEATED PRIEST WITH FACIAL TATTOO, ISLAND OF JAINA
HOLLOW CLAY DOG, COLIMA
HOLLOW CLAY FRAGMENT CENTRAL VERACRUZ
EARTHENWARE DOG VESSEL, COLIMA
CLAY MASK COLIMA
HOLLOW CLAY SEATED MAN FROM COLIMA
HOLLOW CLAY SEATED MAN WITH BOWL AND RATTLE, COLIMA
HOLLOW CLAY SEATED FIGURE WITH DOG, COLIMA

BONE KNIFE WITH GOLD FOIL, GLYPHS
COPPER TURTLE FROM A NECKLACE
STANDING ARCHAIC STYLE FIGURE FROM TLATILCO, MEXICO CITY
EARLY WARRIOR, PAINTED CLAY, TOLTEC
REMOJODAS, CENTRAL VERACRUZ
POTTERY WARRIOR, PROBABLY MAYAN, A.D. 600-900
HOLLOW CLAY SEATED FIGURE, COLIMA
SEATED WOMAN HOLDING BOWL, HOLLOW CLAY, COLIMA
STYLIZED CERAMIC MASK
CLAY DANCER AND ACROBAT, PRE-CLASSIC, 1000 B.C.
BEADS
SEATED MAN WITH HELMET, HOLLOW PAINTED CLAY, NAYARIT
POT WITH EFFIGY HEADS, COLIMA
BEADS
BEADS
HOLLOW CLAY SEATED FIGURE, SHELL NECKLACE, COLIMA
TOY CROCODILE

te Due